PIANO VOCAL GUITAR

THE MICHAEL MASSER COLLECTION

3   DIDN'T WE ALMOST HAVE IT A

8   DO YOU KNOW WHERE YOU'RE GOING TO?

14   FIRST YOU HAVE TO SAY YOU LOVE ME

20   THE GREATEST LOVE OF ALL

17   HOLD ME (IN YOUR ARMS)

24   IF EVER YOU'RE IN MY ARMS AGAIN

29   MISS YOU LIKE CRAZY

34   NOBODY WANTS TO BE ALONE

38   NOTHING'S GONNA CHANGE MY LOVE FOR YOU

44   SAVING ALL MY LOVE FOR YOU

54   TONIGHT, I CELEBRATE MY LOVE

50   TOUCH ME IN THE MORNING

ISBN-13: 978-1-4234-3070-4
ISBN-10: 1-4234-3070-0

HAL•LEONARD®
CORPORATION
7777 W. BLUEMOUND RD. P.O. BOX 13819 MILWAUKEE, WI 53213

Visit Hal Leonard Online at
www.halleonard.com

SONGWRITER/PRODUCER MICHAEL MASSER
first came to fame with "Touch Me in the Morning," the hit power ballad that he wrote and produced for Diana Ross in 1973. With Songwriter Hall of Fame inductee Gerry Goffin he then wrote the Oscar®-nominated "Theme from Mahogany (Do You Know Where You're Going To?)," also for Diana Ross.

Masser later wrote for George Benson (the original version of "The Greatest Love of All"), and also penned the smash R&B duet "Tonight, I Celebrate My Love" for Roberta Flack and Peabo Bryson, as well as "If Ever You're in My Arms Again."

After Teddy Pendergrass scored on the Michael Masser duet "Hold Me (In Your Arms)," with newcomer Whitney Houston, Masser proceeded to compose and produce three Houston chart-toppers, "Saving All My Love for You," "The Greatest Love of All" (with late Songwriters Hall of Fame inductee Linda Creed), and "Didn't We Almost Have It All".

Other collaborations include: Natalie Cole ("Miss You Like Crazy"), Glen Madeiros ("Nothing's Gonna Change My Love for You"), and Barbra Streisand ("Someone That I Used to Love").

Michael Masser was inducted in the Songwriters Hall of Fame on June 7th, 2007.

DIDN'T WE ALMOST HAVE IT ALL

Words and Music by WILL JENNINGS
and MICHAEL MASSER

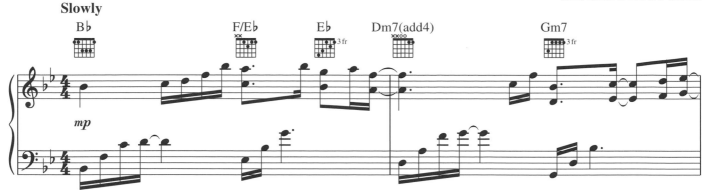

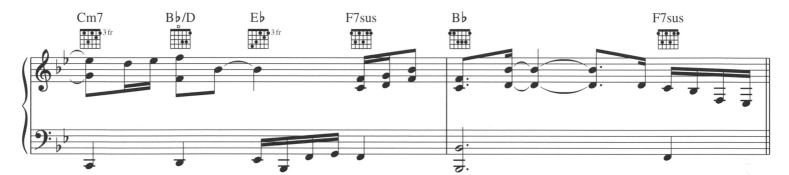

Re-mem-ber when we held on in the rain, the nights we al-most
The way you used to touch me felt so fine; we kept our hearts to-

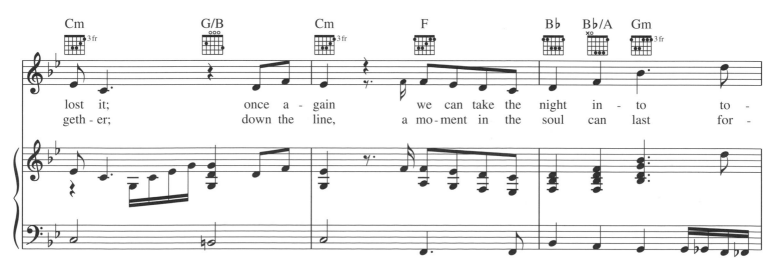

lost it; once a-gain, we can take the night in-to to-
geth-er; down the line, a mo-ment in the soul can last for-

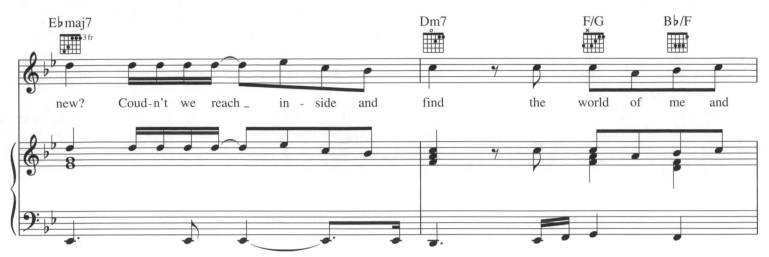

new? Coud-n't we reach _ in - side and find the world of me and

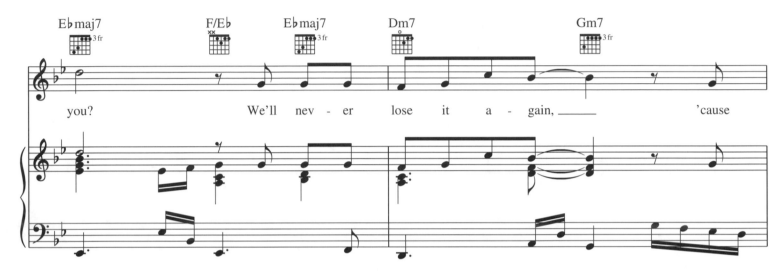

you? We'll nev - er lose it a - gain, _____ 'cause

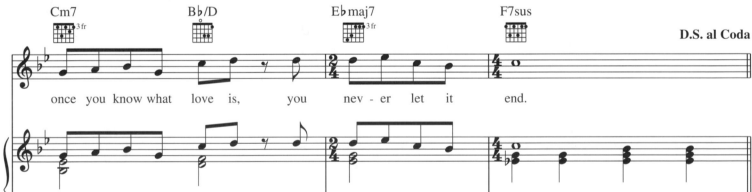

D.S. al Coda

once you know what love is, you nev - er let it end.

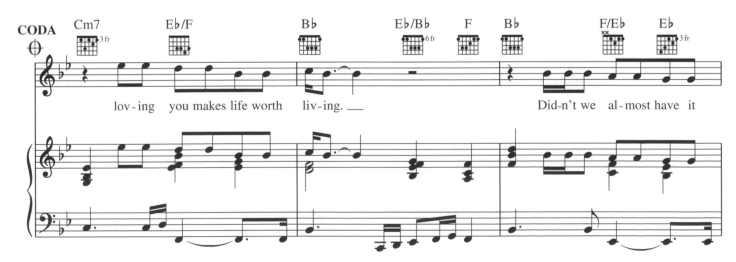

CODA

lov-ing you makes life worth liv-ing. ___ Did-n't we al-most have it

all, the nights we held on till the morn-ing? ___

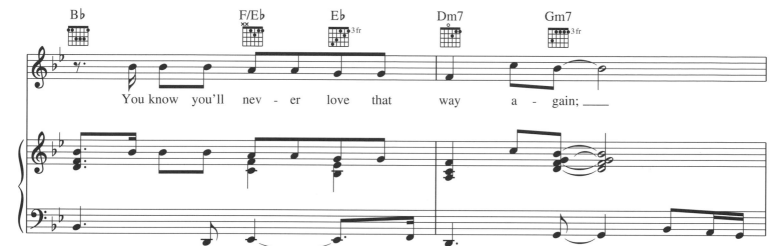

You know you'll nev-er love that way a - gain; ___

did-n't we al-most have it all?

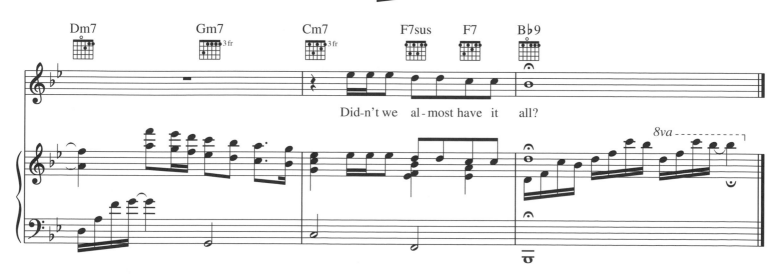

Did-n't we al-most have it all?

DO YOU KNOW WHERE YOU'RE GOING TO?

Theme from MAHOGANY

Words by GERRY GOFFIN
Music by MICHAEL MASSER

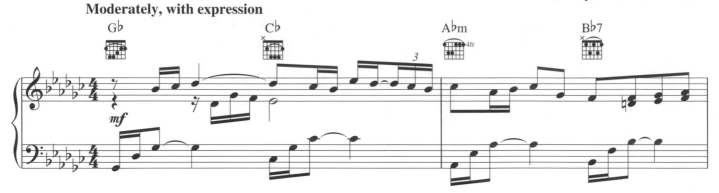

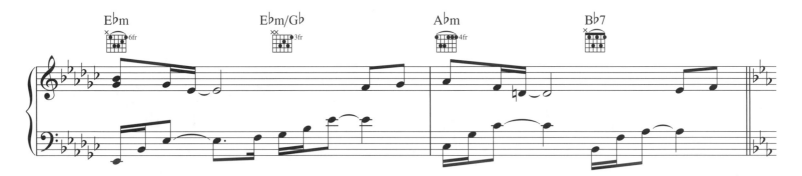

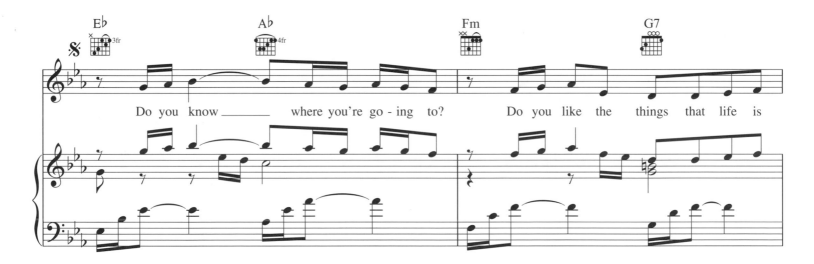

Do you know _____ where you're go-ing to? Do you like the things that life is show-ing you? _____ Where are you go-ing to, do you know?

9

Do you get _____ what you're hop-ing for? When you look be-hind you there's no

o - pen door. _____ What are you hop-ing for, do you

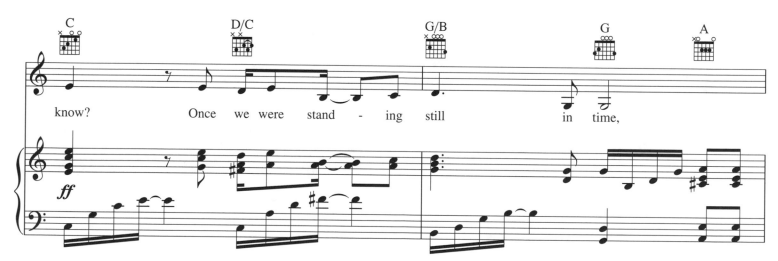

know? Once we were stand - ing still in time,

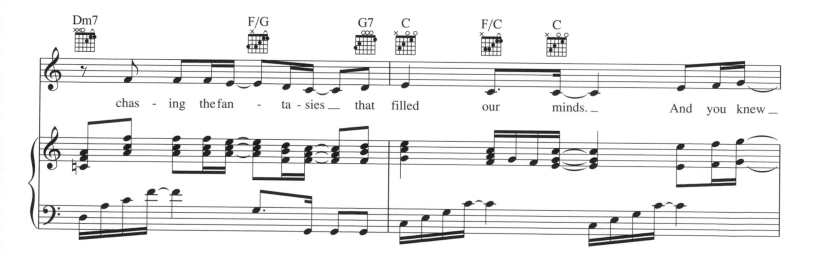

chas-ing the fan - ta - sies _____ that filled our minds. _____ And you knew _____

how I loved you but __ my spir-it was free,

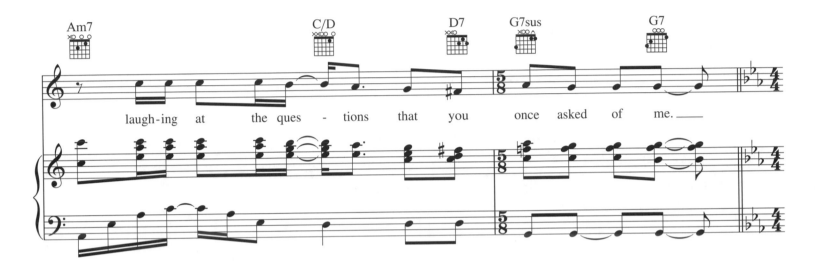

laugh-ing at the ques-tions that you once asked of me. ___

Do you know _____ where you're go-ing to? Do you like the things that life is

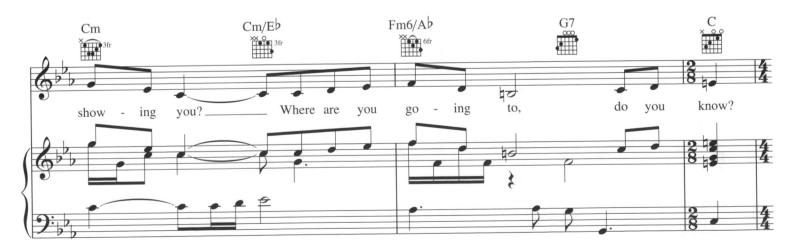

show-ing you? _____ Where are you go-ing to, do you know?

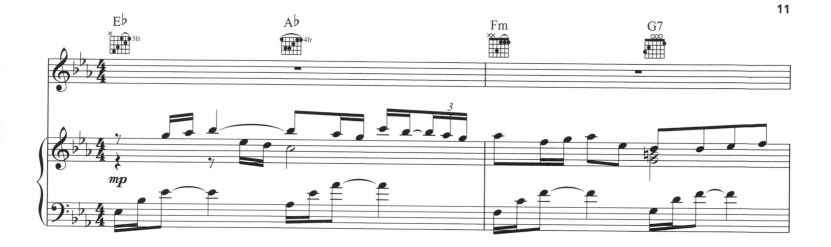

Now ___ look - ing back at all ___ we planned,

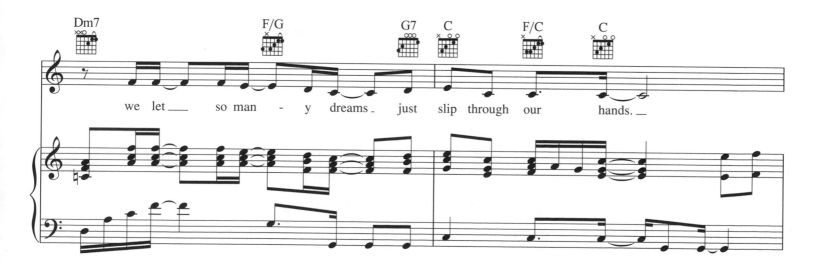

we let ___ so man - y dreams ___ just slip through our hands. ___

Why must _ we wait so long _ be - fore we see

D.S. al Coda

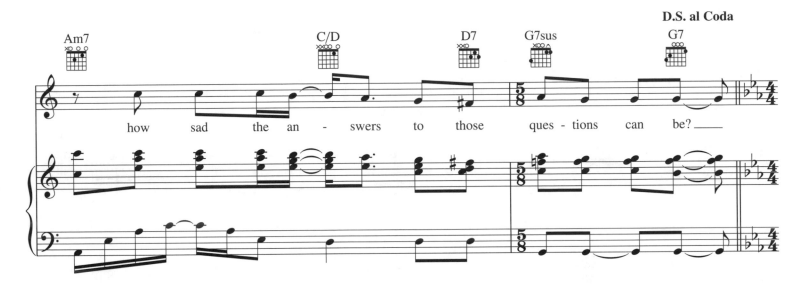

how sad the an - swers to those ques - tions can be? ____

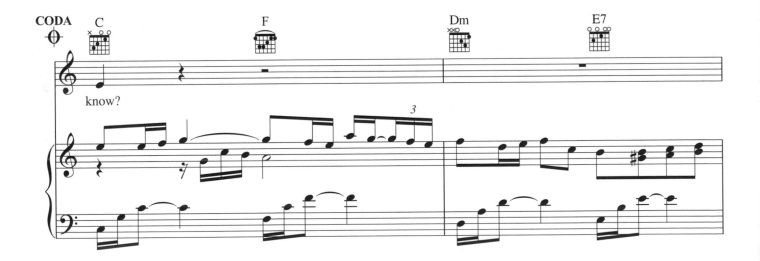

CODA

know?

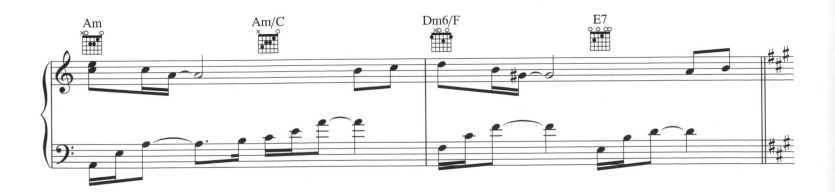

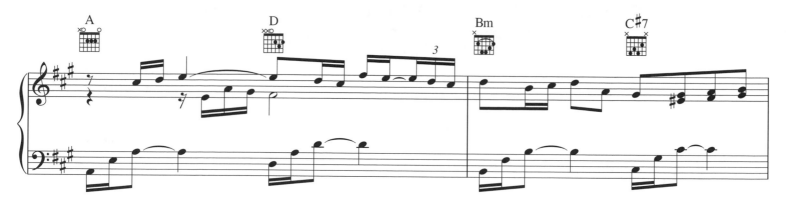

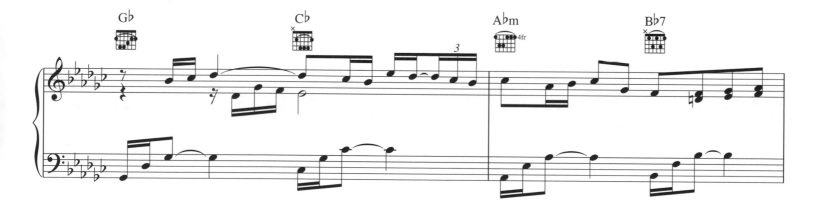

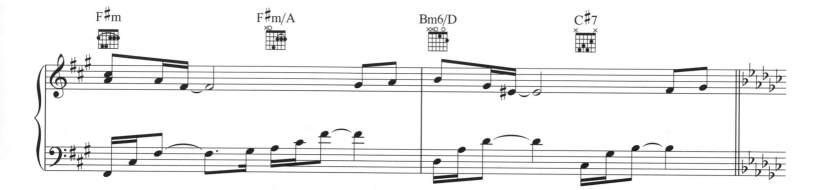

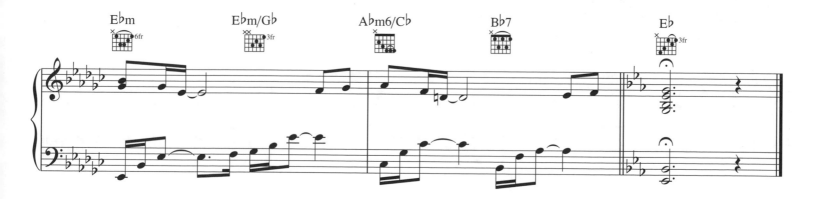

FIRST YOU HAVE TO SAY YOU LOVE ME

Words and Music by MICHAEL MASSER
and NEIL DIAMOND

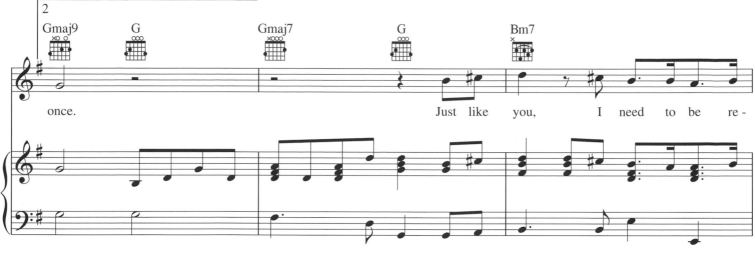

once. Just like you, I need to be re-

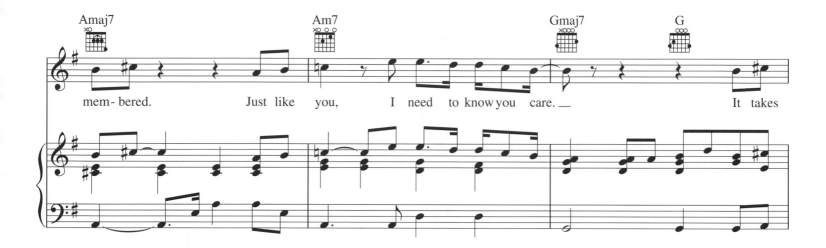

mem- bered. Just like you, I need to know you care. __ It takes

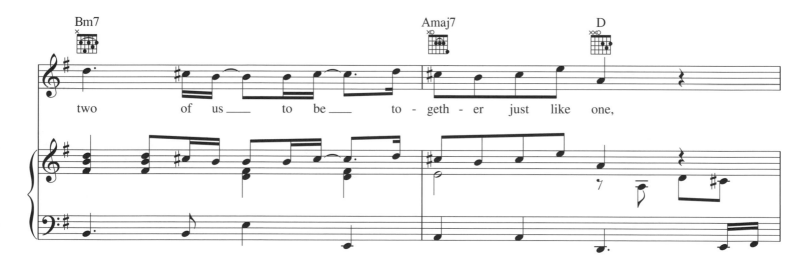

two of us __ to be __ to- geth - er just like one,

D.S. al Coda

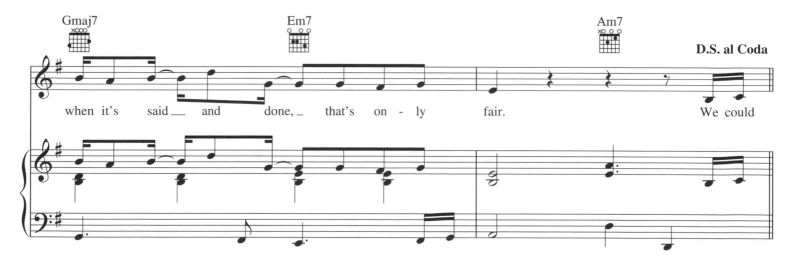

when it's said __ and done, _ that's on - ly fair. We could

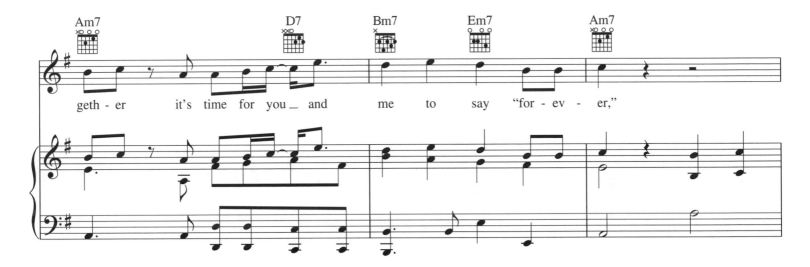

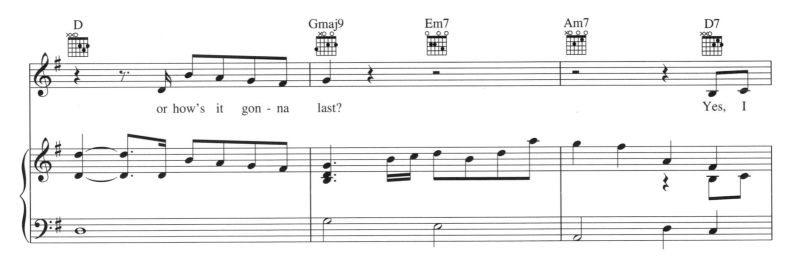

HOLD ME (IN YOUR ARMS)

Words and Music by MICHAEL MASSER
and LINDA CREED

night. *Female:* There's _ some-thing in ___ your eyes, _ I see;   a pure _ and sim - ple hon - est-y. _

___ *(Both:)* Hold me in your arms to - night, _   fill _ my life _

with plea - sure.   Let's not waste this pre - cious time, _

this mo - ment's ours to trea - sure. Hold me in your arms to - night, _

Verse 2:

Female: I believe you, when you say that you love me;
Know that I won't take you for granted.
Tonight the magic has begun.
So won't you hold me touch me,
Make me your woman tonight?

Male: There's something in your eyes I see
I won't betray your trust in me.

THE GREATEST LOVE OF ALL

Words by LINDA CREED
Music by MICHAEL MASSER

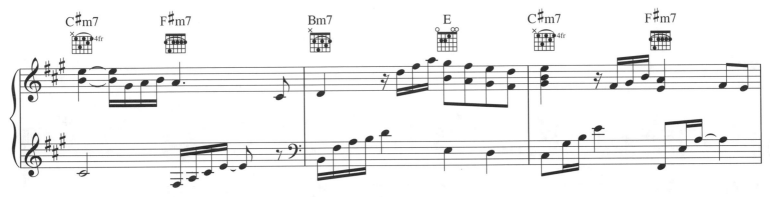

1., D.S. I be-lieve the chil-dren are our fu-ture;
be. 2. Ev-'ry-bod-y's search-ing for a he-ro;

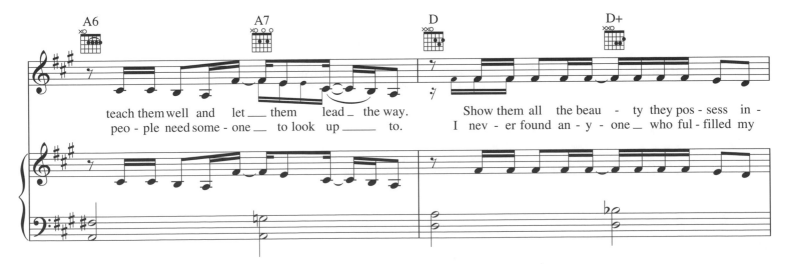

teach them well and let ___ them lead ___ the way.
peo-ple need some-one ___ to look up ___ to.

Show them all the beau-ty they pos-sess in-
I nev-er found an-y-one ___ who ful-filled my

side.
needs.

Give them a sense of pride, to make it eas-i-er; ___ let the chil-dren's
A lone-ly place to be, and so I

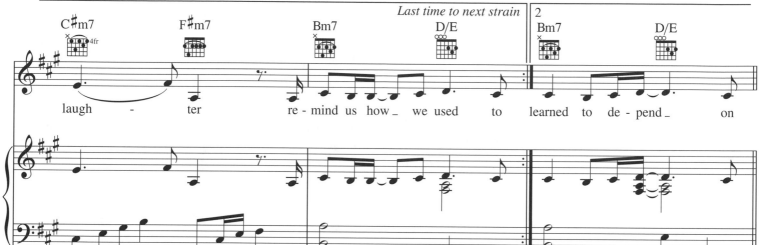

Last time to next strain

laugh - ter re-mind us how ___ we used to
learned to de-pend ___ on

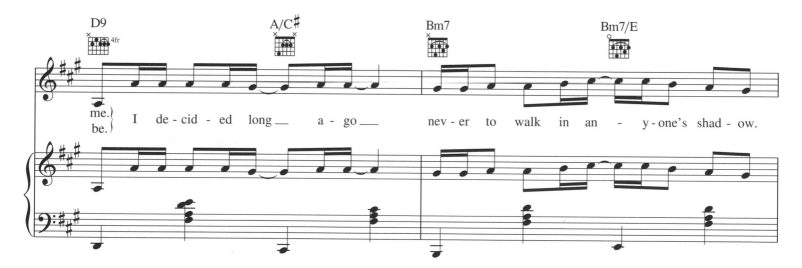

me.
be.

I de-cid-ed long ___ a-go ___ nev-er to walk in an - y-one's shad-ow.

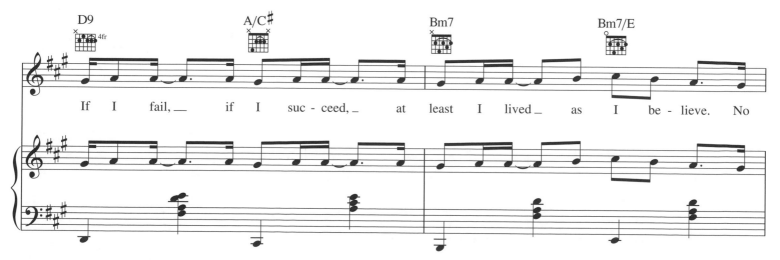

If I fail, ___ if I suc-ceed, ___ at least I lived ___ as I be-lieve. No

IF EVER YOU'RE IN MY ARMS AGAIN

Words and Music by MICHAEL MASSER,
TOM SNOW and CYNTHIA WEIL

It all came so eas - y, all the
I'm see - in' clear - ly how I

lov - in' you gave _ me, the feel - ings we shared. _ And I
still need you near _ me. I still love you so. _ There's _

still can re - mem - ber how your touch was so ten - der. It told me you cared. _
some - thing be - tween us that _ won't ev - er leave _ us. There's no let - ting go. _

We had a once in a life - time, __ but I
We had a once in a life - time, __ but I

just could-n't see it un - til it was gone. __ A sec-ond once in a life -
just did-n't know it till my life fell a - part. __ A sec-ond once in a life -

- time __ may be too much to ask. __ But I swear from now on __ }
- time __ is-n't too much to ask. __ 'Cause I swear from the heart __ }

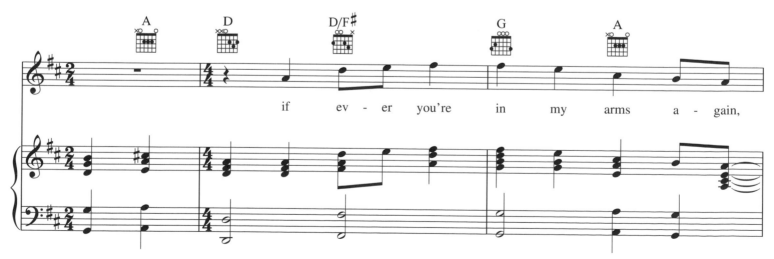

if ev - er you're in my arms a - gain,

this time __ I'll love __ you much bet - ter. If ev - er you're

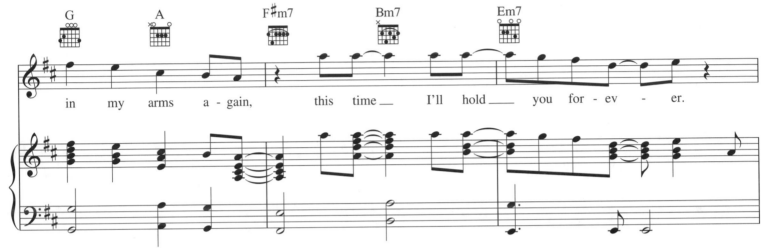

in my arms a - gain, this time __ I'll hold __ you for - ev - er.

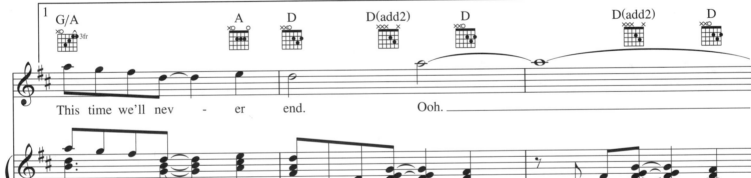

This time we'll nev - er end. Ooh. __

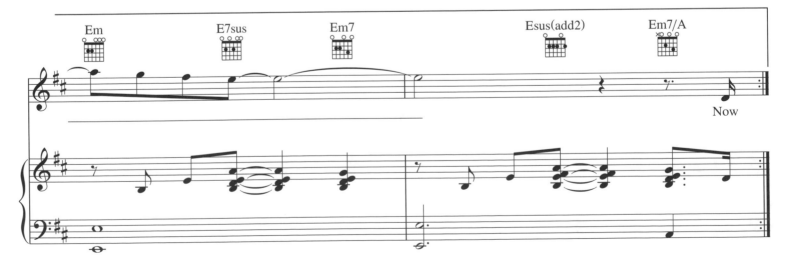

Now

This time we'll nev - er end, _____

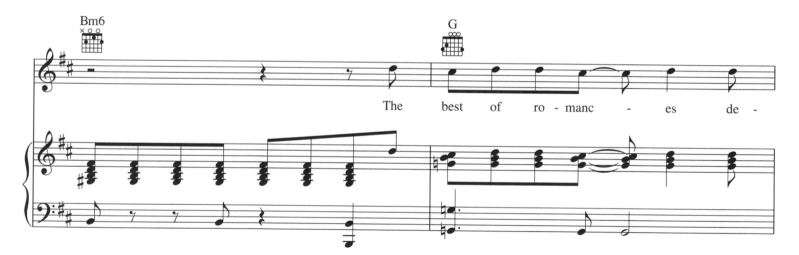

nev - er end. _____

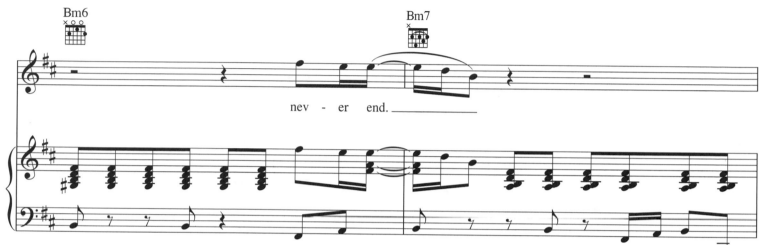

The best of ro - manc - es de -

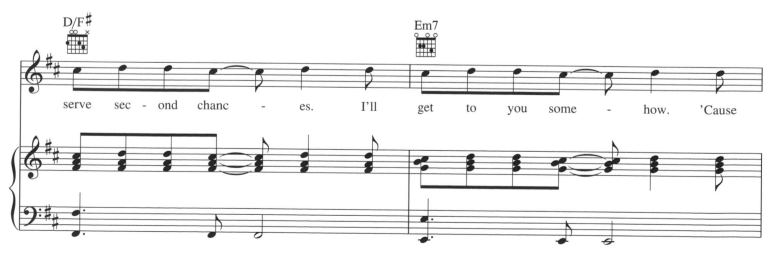

serve sec - ond chanc - es. I'll get to you some - how. 'Cause

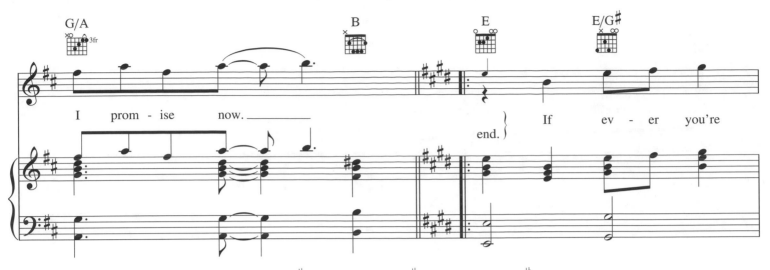

I prom-ise now. _____ end.) If ev-er you're

in my arms a-gain, this time ___ I'll love ___ you much bet - ter.

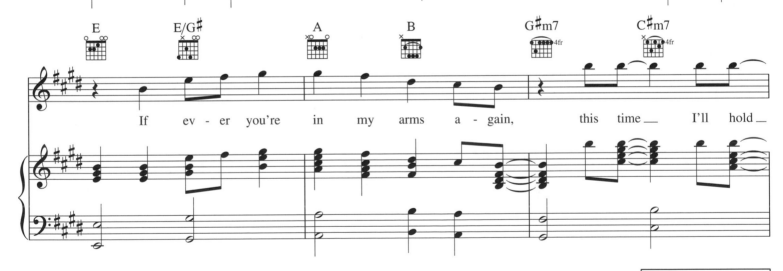

If ev-er you're in my arms a-gain, this time ___ I'll hold ___

Repeat and Fade | **Optional Ending**

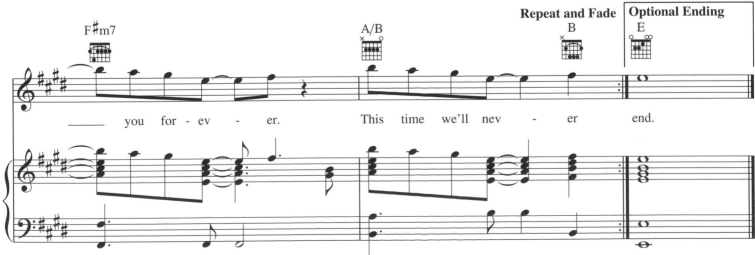

_____ you for-ev - er. This time we'll nev - er end.

MISS YOU LIKE CRAZY

Words and Music by GERRY GOFFIN,
PRESTON GLASS and MICHAEL MASSER

miss you like __ cra - zy. Ev - er since __ you went __ a - way, __

ev - 'ry hour __ of ev - 'ry day. __ I miss you like __ cra - zy, __ I

miss you like __ cra - zy. No mat - ter what __ I say __ or do, __ there's

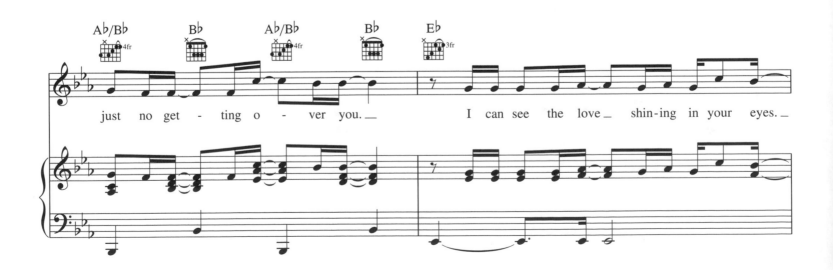

just no get - ting o - ver you. __ I can see the love __ shin - ing in your eyes. __

and it comes as such a sweet sur - prise. It seems be - liev - ing is worth the wait, so

hold me and tell me it's not too late. We're so good to - geth - er, we're start - ing for - ev - er now.

And I miss you like cra - zy, I miss you like cra - zy,

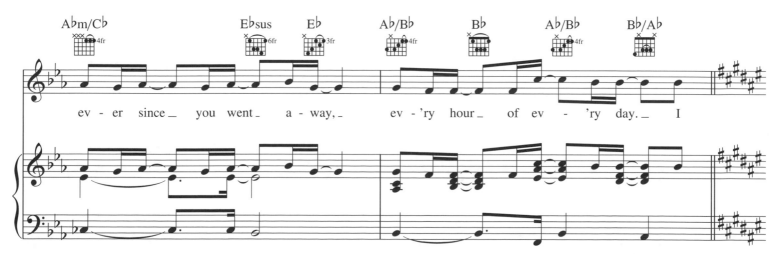

ev - er since you went a - way, ev - 'ry hour of ev - 'ry day. I

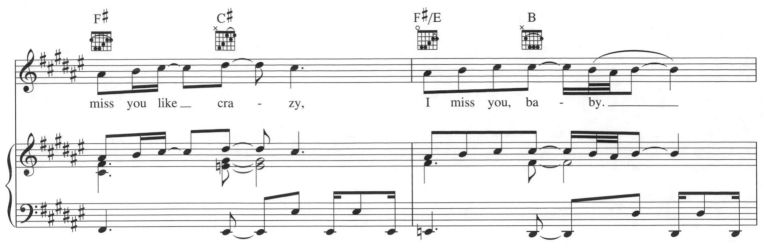

miss you like __ cra - zy, I miss you, ba - by. _____

Love like ours __ will nev - er end, __ just touch me and __ we're there __ a - gain. __

Instrumental solo

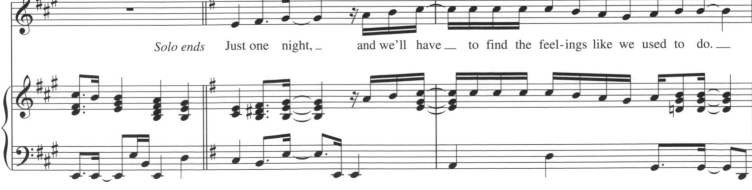

Solo ends Just one night, __ and we'll have __ to find the feel-ings like we used to do. __

Hold on tight, _ and what-ev - er comes our way, we're gon-na make it through. _____ It

seems be - liev - ing is worth the wait, so hold me and tell _ me it's not too late. We're

so good to-geth - er, we're start-ing for ev - er now. ___ And I miss you like _ cra - zy, ___ I

Repeat ad lib. and fade

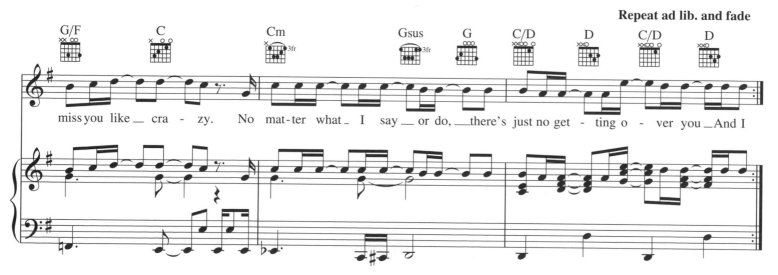

miss you like _ cra - zy. No mat-ter what _ I say _ or do, ___ there's just no get - ting o - ver you _ And I

NOBODY WANTS TO BE ALONE

Words and Music by MICHAEL MASSER
and RHONDA FLEMING

I spent my life, try'n' to tell ev-'ry-one, ___ I've got my-self, I don't

need an-y-one. ___ You heard my words, but you looked in my eyes, ___

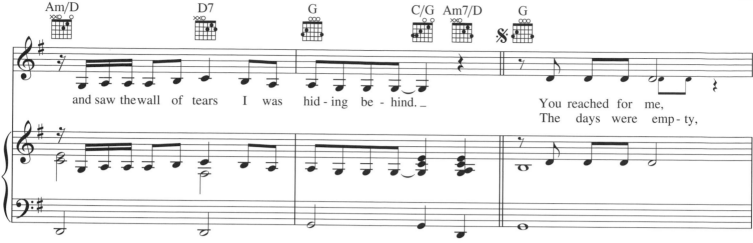

and saw the wall of tears I was hid-ing be-hind. __ You reached for me,
The days were emp-ty,

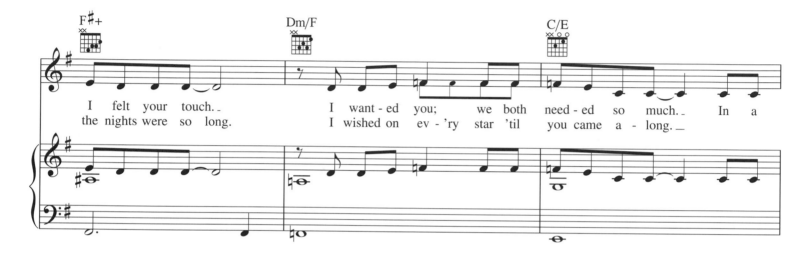

I felt your touch. __ I want-ed you; we both need-ed so much. __ In a
the nights were so long. I wished on ev-'ry star 'til you came a-long. __

world of lone-ly peo-ple, look-in' for love, __ why was I sur-prised to see it
I knew that some-day you'd walk through that door; __ Some-times it's hard, but love is

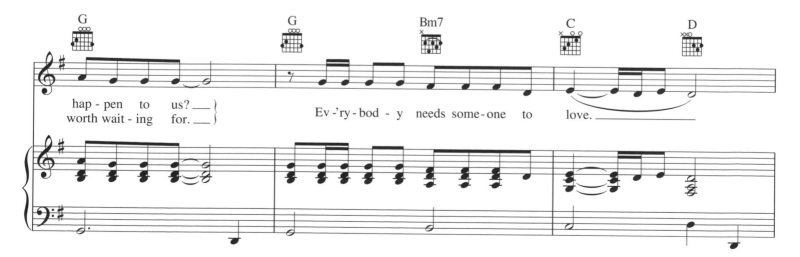

hap-pen to us? __ }
worth wait-ing for. __ }
Ev-'ry-bod-y needs some-one to love. __

Ev-'ry-bod-y wants to love _ some-one when the nights are long _ and cold. Ev-'ry-bod-y needs some-one to

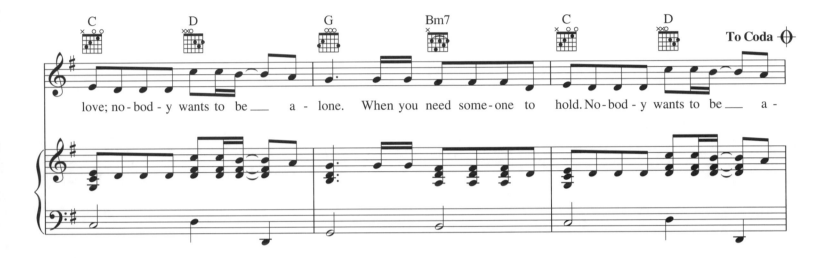

love; no-bod-y wants to be __ a - lone. When you need some-one to hold. No-bod-y wants to be __ a-

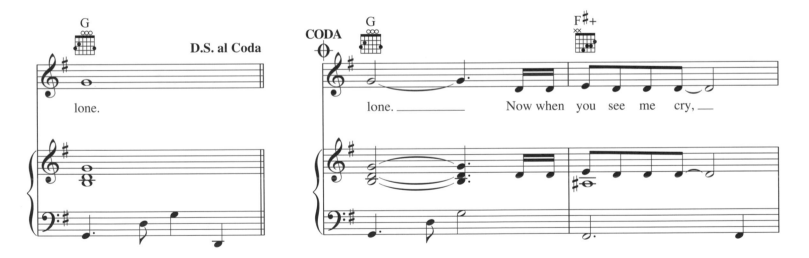

lone.

D.S. al Coda

CODA

lone. _____ Now when you see me cry, __

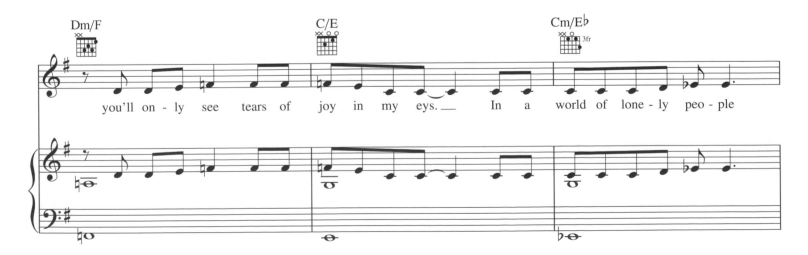

you'll on - ly see tears of joy in my eys. __ In a world of lone - ly peo - ple

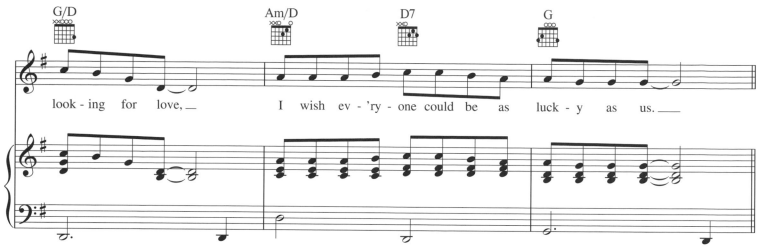

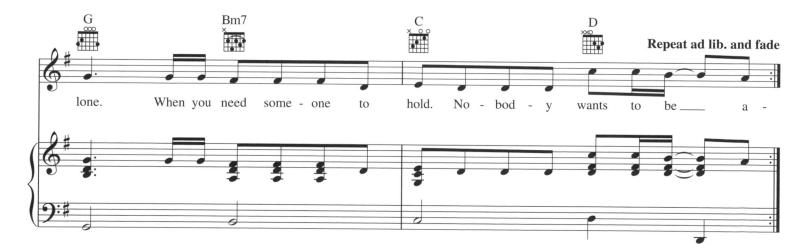

NOTHING'S GONNA CHANGE MY LOVE FOR YOU

Words and Music by GERRY GOFFIN
and MICHAEL MASSER

Slow Ballad

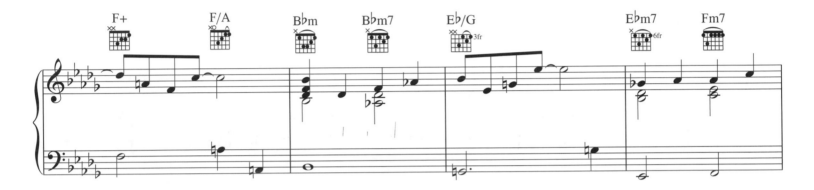

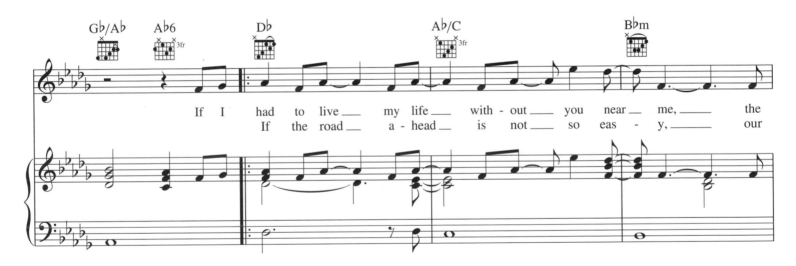

If I had to live ___ my life ___ with - out ___ you near ___ me, ___ the

If the road ___ a - head ___ is not ___ so eas - y, ___ our

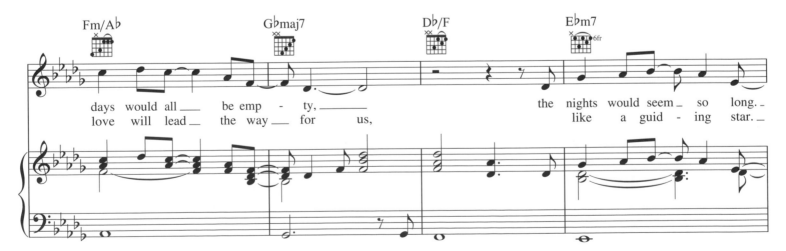

days would all ___ be emp - ty, ___ the nights would seem ___ so long. ___

love will lead ___ the way ___ for us, like a guid - ing star. ___

With you I see ___ for-ev- ___ er, oh, ___ so clear-ly. ___ I
I'll be there ___ for you ___ if you ___ should need ___ me. ___

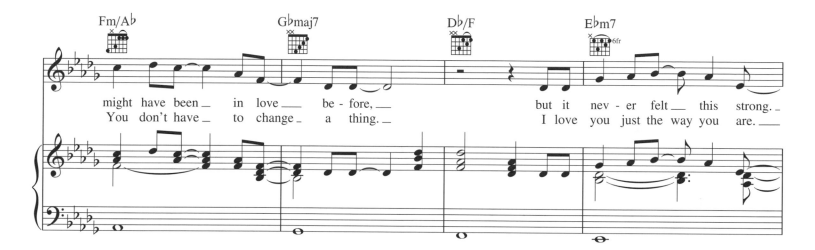

might have been ___ in love ___ be-fore, ___ but it nev-er felt ___ this strong. _
You don't have ___ to change _ a thing. ___ I love you just the way you ___ are. ___

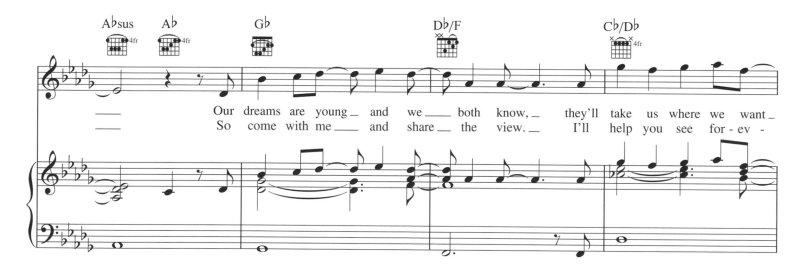

___ Our dreams are young _ and we ___ both know, ___ they'll take us where we want _
___ So come with me ___ and share ___ the view. ___ I'll help you see for-ev-

___ to go. ___ }
- er, too. ___ } Hold me now, _ touch me now, _ I don't want to live _

with - out you. ___ Noth-ing's gon - na change my love ___ for you. ___ You

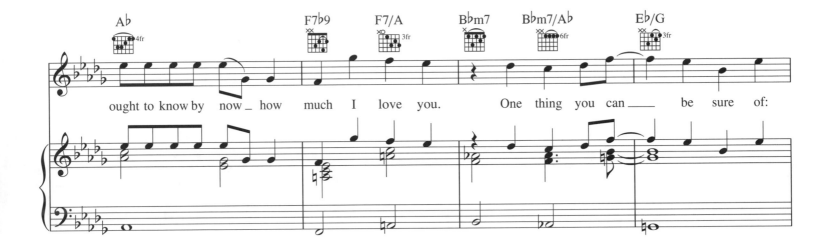

ought to know by now ___ how much I love you. One thing you can ___ be sure of:

I'll nev-er ask for more ___ than your love. Noth-ing's gon - na change my love ___ for you. ___ You

ought to know by now ___ how much I love you. The world may change my whole ___ life through but

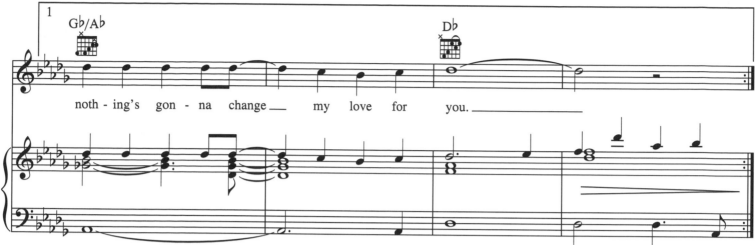

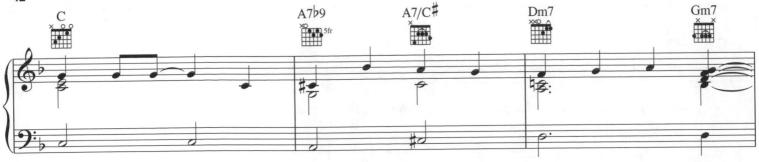

Noth-ing's gon - na change my love ___ for you. ___ You ought to know by now ___ how
you.

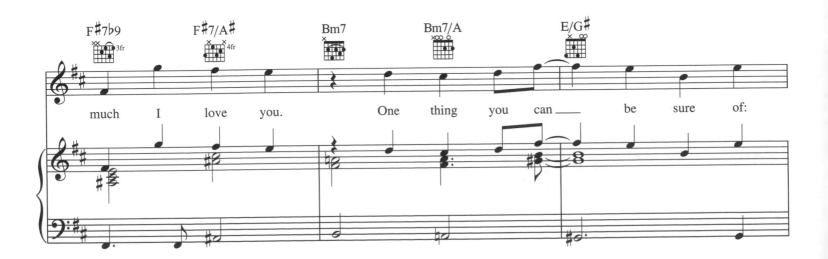

much   I   love   you.   One   thing   you   can ___ be   sure   of:

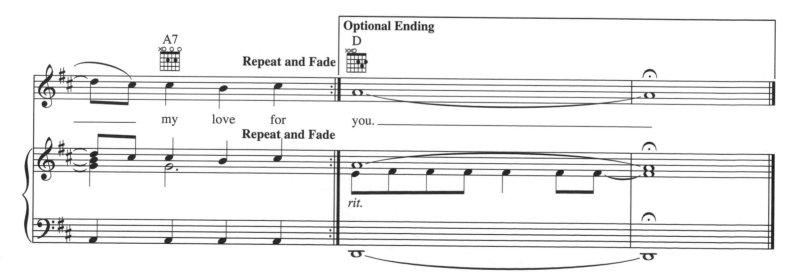

SAVING ALL MY LOVE FOR YOU

Words by GERRY GOFFIN
Music by MICHAEL MASSER

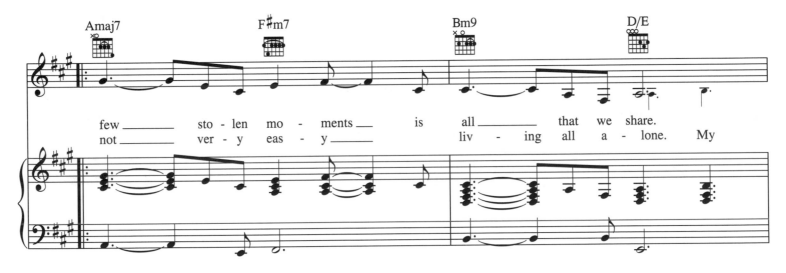

few ____ sto - len mo - ments ____ is all ____ that we share.
not ____ ver - y eas - y ____ liv - ing all a - lone. My

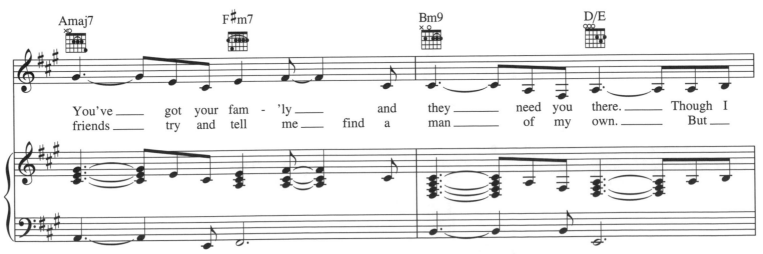

You've ____ got your fam - 'ly ____ and they ____ need you there. ____ Though I
friends ____ try and tell me ____ find a man ____ of my own. ____ But ____

F#m7   B/F#   F#m7   B/F#

try ____ to re - sist ____ be - ing last ____ on your list,   but
each ____ time I try, ____ I just break ____ down and cry, 'cause I'd

A   F#m7   G#m7   C#9

no oth - er man's ____ gon - na do, _____ so I'm
rath - er be home ____ feel - in' blue, _____

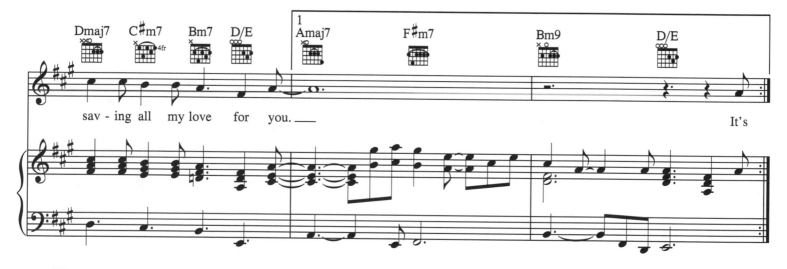

Dmaj7   C#m7   Bm7   D/E   **1** Amaj7   F#m7   Bm9   D/E

sav - ing all my love for you. ___   It's

2 A   G#m7   C#7

___   You used to tell __ me __ we'd

run a-way to-geth-er; ___ love gives you the right ___ to be

free. ___ You said, ___ "Be pa - tient, ___ just

wait a lit - tle long - er," ___ but that's just ___ an old fan - ta -

sy. ___ I've got ___ to get read - y ___ just a

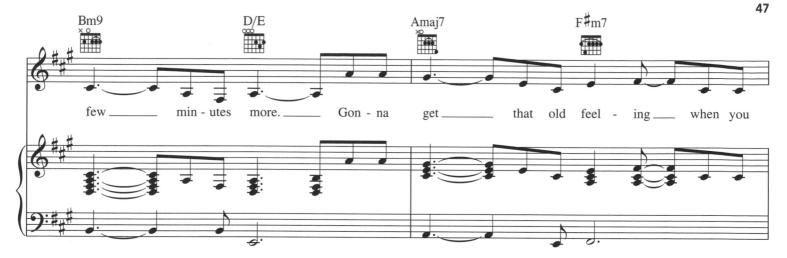

few _____ min - utes more. _____ Gon - na get _____ that old feel - ing ____ when you

walk _____ through that door. _____ 'Cause to - night _____ is the night _____ for ____

feel - ing all right. _____ We'll be mak - ing love the whole night ____

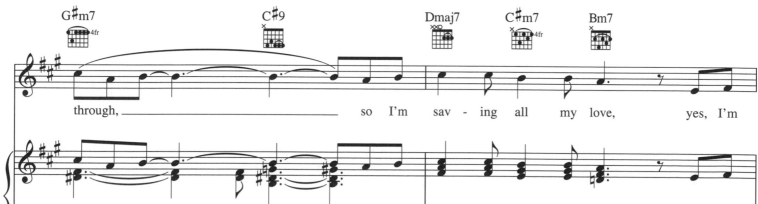

through, _____ so I'm sav - ing all my love, yes, I'm

saving all my love, yes, I'm saving all my love for ___ you. _____

___ No oth - er wom - an ___ is

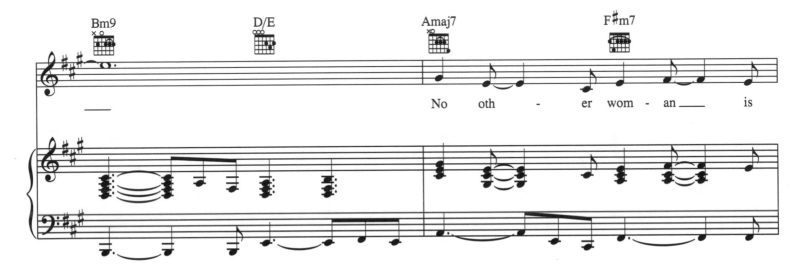

gon - na love you more. _____ 'Cause to - night ___ is the night ___ that I'm

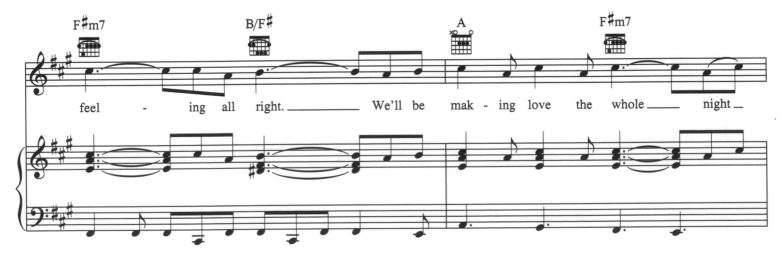

feel - ing all right. _____ We'll be mak - ing love the whole ___ night ___

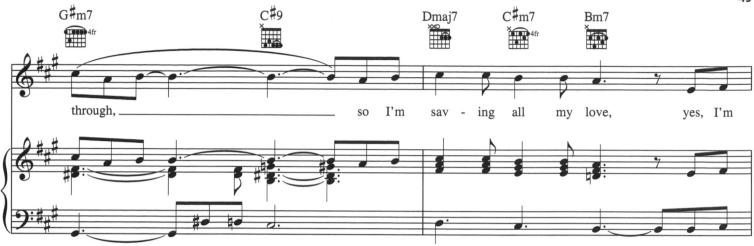

through, _____ so I'm sav - ing all my love, yes, I'm

sav - ing all my lov - ing, ___ yes, I'm sav - ing all my love for

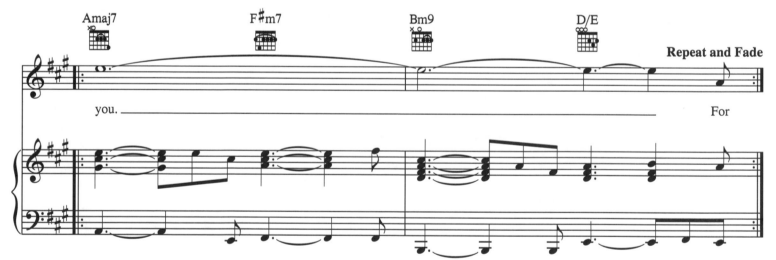

Repeat and Fade

you. _____ For

Optional Ending

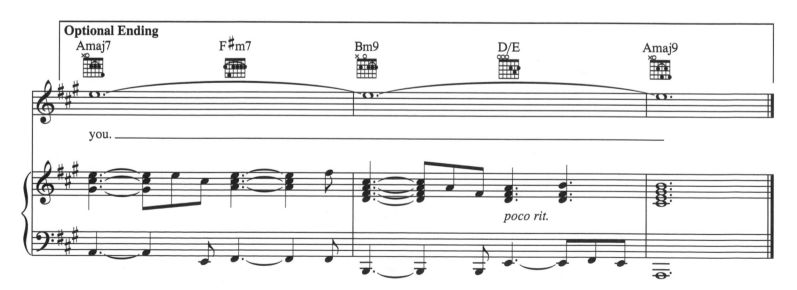

you. _____

poco rit.

TOUCH ME IN THE MORNING

Words and Music by RONALD MILLER
and MICHAEL MASSER

TONIGHT, I CELEBRATE MY LOVE

Music by MICHAEL MASSER
Lyric by GERRY GOFFIN

Slowly and expressively

To -

night _____ I cel - e - brate my love _____ for you; _____ it seems _____ the nat - u - ral
night _____ I cel - e - brate my love _____ for you; _____ and hope _____ that deep in - side you
night _____ I cel - e - brate my love _____ for you; _____ and soon _____ this old world will

thing _____ to do. To - night _____ no one's gon - na find us, _____ we'll leave the world be -
feel _____ it too. To - night _____ our spir - its will be climb - ing to a sky lit up _____ with
seem _____ brand-new. To - night _____ we will both dis - cov - er _____ how friends turn in - to

hind us, _____ when I make love to you. _ To-
dia - monds _ when I make
lov - ers, _____ when I make

night. To - love to you. _ To-

To next strain

night _____ I cel - e - brate my love for you _ and the

mid-night sun _____ is gon - na come shin - ing through. _ To-

night _____ there'll be no dis-tance be - tween us.

What I want

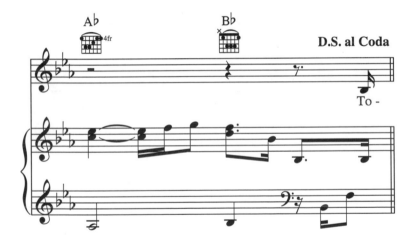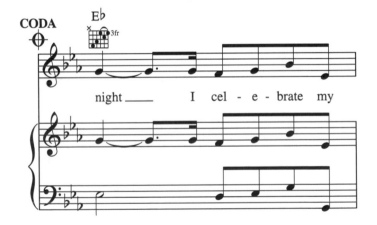

most to do __ is to get close to you __ to - night.

To - night I cel - e - brate my

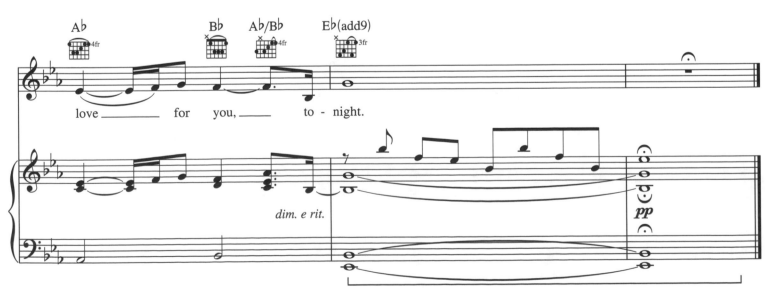

love _____ for you, _____ to - night.